- 2

The Small-Business Guide to Creating Your
Employee  Handbook

The Small-Business Guide to Creating Your Employee* Handbook

Kimberley King, BA, CHRP

Self-Counsel Press
(a division of)
International Self-Counsel Press Ltd.
Canada   USA

Self-Counsel Press acknowledges the financial support of the Government of Canada through the Canada Book Fund for our publishing activities.

First edition: 2014

Library and Archives Canada Cataloguing in Publication

King, Kimberley, 1976-, author

    The small business guide to creating your employee handbook / Kimberley King, BA, CHRP.

ISBN 978-1-77040-201-0 (pbk.)

    1. Employee handbooks. I. Title.

HF5549.5.E423K55 2014   658.4'55   C2014-901050-8

Self-Counsel Press
(a division of)
International Self-Counsel Press Ltd.

North Vancouver, BC
Canada

Contents

Samples

Notice to Readers

The information contained in this Guide is not legal advice and should not be relied upon as such.

Laws are constantly changing. Every effort is made to keep this publication as current as possible. However, the author, the publisher, and the vendor of this book make no representations or warranties regarding the outcome or the use to which the information in this book is put and are not assuming any liability for any claims, losses, or damages arising out of the use of this book. Please be sure that you have the most recent edition.

Employment standards and human rights legislation also varies considerably by province. You should have independent legal counsel review your handbook once completed, to ensure that it works for your business requirements and complies with employment standards and human rights laws for the province in which you operate. Not all employees are covered by all employment standards requirements. You should consult a lawyer to find out whether some or all of your employees may be exempt from all or some of such requirements.

Human rights legislation applies to all employers and may impact how any given policy set out in this book may be lawfully implemented.

Dedication

This book is dedicated to my wonderful family, who encouraged me to write this book, and then gave me the time to do it. In particular I'd like to acknowledge my husband, who gives me so much strength, love, and support every day.

Introduction

Imagine that it's 11:00 a.m. on a Tuesday and you've been in your office for two hours now. All of your employees are hard at work at their desks; at least you think they are. Lindsey seems to spend a lot of time on her Facebook account thinking you don't notice, and Harold has just emailed you that he needs to take some time off for personal reasons and he wants to know if he can still get paid for those days. Not to mention that Sam hasn't shown up for work yet, even though you thought it was an unspoken rule that everyone starts work at 9:00 a.m. sharp. Now what? You are focused on running your small business, but these "people issues" are starting to interfere.

As your business grows, your employee base will likely grow, and so will the amount of human resource issues that can challenge, frustrate, delight, reward, and exasperate you. You are not a human resources expert or consultant, and your business is not yet at the scale where it needs an in-house human resources professional. And yet you can and will be presented with these obstacles and issues. So how do you begin to address them?

Creating an employee handbook is a great place to start! A handbook should tell new and existing employees what the basic laws are in Canada governing their pay, vacation, leaves, and health and safety issues. It should outline any policies that are specific to your company, and address policies that govern all workplaces such as harassment and discrimination policies. It is a document that will help guide your employees and provide valuable general information about your policies, programs, and expectations. Having fair and consistent policies and programs in one document ensures that both employees and managers are on the same page, and feel like they are being dealt with in a fair and consistent manner. In general, it will help you answer a lot of questions that your employees will have about their employment now, and in the future, and will allow everyone to be more productive at work.

1. How to Use This Guide to Create the Right Handbook for Your Company

Please note that this handbook will not work for everyone. Unionized employees and employees who work for federally regulated employers are governed by different rules and regulations, and this book was not written to encompass those areas; nor can this book be used in the United States or other countries. This handbook is specifically meant for provincially regulated, small- to medium-sized, privately held businesses operating within Canada.

Creating a handbook from scratch can be an overwhelming and time-consuming process, especially if you are unfamiliar with employment standards legislation and human resources best practices. That is why I have created one for you: A basic template to customize to your particular business! Each chapter represents a section that you should include in your handbook, although it by no means covers every area and you should adapt the handbook to your own business requirements. For some policies, I have given you options (A, B, C) to choose from, and I have provided some of the basic language that can be used as well as templates (on the CD included with this book) to get you started. Once you have completed the templates and formed your own handbook, I recommend having an employment lawyer in the province in which you operate review it to ensure your legal requirements have been met.

The response to almost any employee-related question you might ask an HR professional will likely be, "Did you document it?" This means, is there anything written in regards to the employee situation with which you are dealing? Documentation is the cornerstone of the human resources profession and it shows that the employer is doing his or her due diligence when it comes to employees. An employee handbook should be the beginning of that documentation process.

My recommendation in getting started would be to buy a ringed binder for each of your employees so that each person can have a copy of your employee handbook; keep a few extra on hand for any new employees, too. Some companies I know do have their handbook in electronic format only, but you will want to seek the advice of legal counsel in the province(s) in which you conduct business if you decide to put it solely in electronic form, as legally it may not be as acceptable as a printed document.

Then follow along with the sections below, creating your handbook and starting each new policy on its own page. That way, if you need to update only part of the policy at a later date, you do not need to print the whole handbook again, just that one page with the specific policy on it. On the same note, there is no need to number the pages in your handbook, as you will have to update certain policies in the future and numbering pages will mean you will have to reprint the whole document. Instead, use chapters to number your policies (e.g., "1:4" would be the fourth policy in the first chapter). This will make it a much easier process when you go to update and print your policies. I have not numbered the templates for you, as some policies will be included for some companies, but not all; you can customize the templates and number the ones you use to suit your company.

I recommend putting the current date on your handbook, at the bottom of each page, so that you have a reference to the last time it was updated. Ensure you change the date each time you update your handbook. For example, say you decide to update the page on your group benefits, so you remove that one page and print off a new one with the updated information. At the bottom of the page, you would write "Updated: January 2015." This way your employees will know it's new information too.

Another suggestion for putting your handbook together is to include a table of contents. After your employees have read through the handbook once, they likely will only go back to the handbook for specific questions on company policies. You will want to make it easy for them to reference and find the material.

1
About This Employee Handbook

It is important that your employees are given an opportunity to read your handbook during paid company time, and that they sign an acknowledgement form stating that they have read and understood it. The reason for this goes back to the importance of documentation in any employee situation.

Misunderstandings and unreasonable employee expectations can arise if there isn't a reliable handbook for new and existing employees to reference. Also, if there is no proof that an employee has read and understood a company's policies, then problems can occur. If an employee has read, understood, and signed the agreement that he or she has read and understood the policies, but continues to defy your dress code policy, then you have already done some of your due diligence toward "performance managing" his or her behaviour. It will be difficult for a person to say "I didn't know I couldn't wear shorts to work," when he or she has already signed your employee handbook acknowledgement form which states that he or she has read the handbook, which states that shorts are not allowed. It will also be very clear to your other employees that you aren't trying to discipline or terminate one employee based on something frivolous or a policy that was never clearly communicated. Your handbook, once rolled out to your staff, will reassure them they are being dealt with fairly.

The very first page in your handbook could be titled "About the Handbook," or "Important Notice about Your Handbook," and contain the notice and Confirmation of Acknowledgement in Sample 1.

It is important that this Acknowledgement is signed, dated, and placed in the each employee's file. I had an employee once who told me that she didn't know the staff discount was for staff members only, when we caught her purchasing items for her friends. I was able to pull out her Employee Acknowledgement form, which she had signed stating that she read and understood the policies in the handbook, namely that the staff discount was for staff only. She had no option but to admit she had violated a company policy, and we were able to have a straightforward performance management discussion at that point. But without her signed form, it would have been a "he said, she said" discussion that would have made the problem very difficult to address.

Sample 1
About the Handbook

Your new employee handbook was created to provide you, as an employee of *(Company)*, with the information you need to understand our company culture and policies. This handbook supersedes any earlier policy material.

This handbook is not a contract of employment, nor a guarantee of any kind. It offers an overview of our company and employment policies. In the event that something in this handbook conflicts with federal or provincial laws, those laws will govern.

We at *(Company)* reserve the right to edit, alter, or otherwise change policies and passages in this handbook at any time, without prior notice to employees.

If you have any questions in regards to this handbook, please see your manager.

Confirmation and Acknowledgement of Receipt

It is a requirement for all employees to read and abide by this employee handbook. You are expected to read the employee handbook during working hours and return a signed copy of acknowledgement to your manager.

I, _____, acknowledge that I have read, understood and will abide by the policies in the Employee Handbook:

_____   _____
Signature   Date

2
Start Your Handbook with a Welcoming Introduction

Once you've taken care of the formalities involved in the first section (the notice and acknowledgement of receipt), you are ready to really get the ball rolling!

The next page of your handbook is going to set the tone for your document, so some thought needs to be put into the introduction. Will it be a straightforward, no-nonsense handbook, or a casual, laid-back handbook? Will it be serious, or lighthearted, or somewhere in the middle? The language you use is important, as it needs to reflect your company culture and how you want your policies and programs to be viewed by your employees. This will likely be the first document your new employees will read about your company, so you will want it to not only educate them but also inspire and motivate them (or at the very least, make them feel they have joined a company that has its stuff together).

An introduction with a welcome note and the history of how the company started can be a nice way to begin, as this can be kept light and short. If the company has a mission and/or vision statement, this would be a great place to include it, along with anything else that adds to or enhances the perception of company culture or speaks to the day-to-day details of working for your company.

There is an example of a welcome or introduction page in Sample 2. While this is just a brief example of a welcome page, much more creativity can be included here. For example, adding interesting graphics, your company logo, or a friendly letter from the company owner can all set the tone of your company culture. You could also add in an organizational chart if you feel it would be helpful to new employees. You will (and should) spend the majority of the time spent on this handbook on the welcome page, as the other sections don't allow for the same degree of creativity or leeway.

Sample 2
Welcome Page

Welcome to Candles for You Company!

We are so excited that you have joined us! We are a small (but growing) company that began in 2008 with one basic, white, battery-operated candle as our test model, and now we have over 40 different styles and colours of candles, selling in over 300 stores across Canada. We are looking forward to continuing this journey with you and seeing where the future will take us!

The owners, Karen and Jess, began experimenting with wax and candles when they were 5 and 7 years old respectively, in their mother's house. They loved melting different colors of wax together, although one experiment almost burned down their mother's curtains! Thirty years later, the sisters created Candles for You Company, when they noticed a need in the market for candles that looked, smelled and felt real, but that could be turned on by a battery instead of fire, and therefore were completely safe around children and pets.

Our *mission* is to provide beautiful looking and smelling candles that seem to burn like real candles, without any danger.

Our *vision* is to set the world on fire with our energy, enthusiasm, and lifelike candles.

At Candles for You Company, Karen and Jess value the visionary thinking, enthusiasm, and energy of their employees and consider these the core values for their company.

Our company has one head office location in Vancouver, BC, as well as one small warehouse located in East Vancouver, BC. We have approximately 20 employees working for us full time. Upon starting with us at Candles for You Company, you will be asked to spend a week working in the warehouse so that you have a full understanding of how our candles are made and shipped to our clients. We feel that this will empower our employees and improve our processes going forward. We welcome any and all suggestions for improvement!

Our company also gives back to the community in which it operates. We are very involved with the local United Way and we give employees one paid day per year off to volunteer in the community, through the United Way. In addition, 1% of every sale we make at Candles for You Company goes to our local United Way. We are thrilled you are able to help us make a difference in our community for people in need.

"We are a small company that will make a big impact. It is because of our dedicated employees that we have the dynamic, quickly growing company that we have today."

— Karen and Jess

So again, welcome to Candles for You Company. We hope you are here for a good time AND a long time!

3
Employment Policies

There are certain policies that are clear-cut and need to be included in every handbook, and these are the policies that address disability accommodations; discrimination, harassment (including sexual harassment), bullying, and human rights. These are the sections to include in your handbook in Samples 3, 4, and 5.

Sample 3
Disability Accommodations Policy

(Company) is committed to ensuring equal opportunity in employment for qualified individuals with disabilities. *(Company)* complies with all applicable laws regarding the employment and accommodation of people with disabilities.

Reasonable accommodation is available to an employee with a disability if the disability affects the performance of job functions. Any employee who feels he or she needs such accommodation should contact his or her manager to discuss such accommodation.

Sample 4
Discrimination, Harassment, and Bullying Policy

(Company) is committed to creating and maintaining a workplace that is free from discrimination, harassment, and bullying. *(Company)* adheres to applicable provincial and territorial laws prohibiting harassment, discrimination, and bullying, and such conduct will not be tolerated at *(Company)*. Any employee found to have engaged in harassment, discrimination, or bullying may be subject to discipline up to and including termination. This policy applies to all employees, consultants, customers, and vendors of *(Company)*.

Harassment or bullying occurs when a person or group is subjected to comments or conduct that is hostile, insulting, or demeaning, or is otherwise offensive and such conduct is known, or should reasonably be known, to be unwelcome. Harassment and bullying can be physical or psychological. Common examples of harassment include name-calling, sending offensive emails, pranks, offensive joke-telling, and making offensive gestures. Harassment occurs when a person's conduct has the effect of harassing someone; it does not matter whether the person intended to offend or insult the other person.

Harassment can be a form of human rights discrimination. In BC for example, the British Columbia *Human Rights Code* in effect prohibits harassment in the workplace on several grounds, including race, colour, ancestry, place of origin, political belief, religion, marital or family status, sex, sexual orientation, physical and/or mental disability, or age.

Sexual Harassment

Sexual harassment is a form of discrimination and occurs when someone is subjected to unwelcome sexual or gender-related remarks, gestures, or other verbal or physical behaviour of a sexual nature. This can include, but is not limited to:

- Unwanted touching or physical contact.

- Making offensive jokes or remarks about women or men.

- Displaying sexually offensive pictures.

- Making sexual requests or suggestions.

- Offering employment benefits in exchange for sexual favours.

- Written communications of a sexual nature (on paper, whiteboards, over email, or via instant messaging, among other possibilities).

- Retaliating or threatening to retaliate after a negative response to harassment or for threatening to report or reporting harassment.

Sexual harassment isn't always sexual in nature; it can happen when someone harasses someone else simply because he or she is a man or woman. It can also include physical contact or words of a sexual nature that are intended to create an intimidating or hostile environment, or that are intended to affect someone's work performance, advancement opportunities, or otherwise create an intolerable work environment.

Sample 4 – Continued

Employees should at all times behave in a professional and respectful manner and avoid any behaviour that might be deemed questionable.

Reporting Procedure

As an employee of *(Company)*, at no point are you expected to tolerate any form of harassment or bullying while at work or involved in company business. If you experience harassment, bullying, or discrimination, or believe that someone has violated this policy, you should immediately report the incident to your manager and/or the owner of *(Company)* as soon as possible.

(Company) will review the complaint, investigate the allegations, and determine whether the conduct complained of constitutes harassment or bullying, and will discipline any person found to be in violation of this harassment and bullying policy. *(Company)* will do its best to protect the identity and confidentiality of those involved to the extent allowable by law and the need to investigate and resolve any complaints or issues.

If an employee makes a harassment, bullying, or discrimination complaint in bad faith, or retaliates against any individual who makes a complaint, that employee may be disciplined, up to and including termination.

Sample 5
Human Rights Policy

(Company) respects the human rights of its employees, customers, and vendors, and we comply with all applicable human rights laws in the province(s) in which we operate.

Applicable human rights laws will be followed in our hiring, compensation, discipline, and termination practices, and in all other aspects of the employment relationship. We do not unlawfully discriminate based on race, colour, ancestry, place of origin, religion, marital or family status, sex, sexual orientation, disability, age, or any other classification protected under the applicable law. Our decisions are based on merit, business needs, and bona fide occupational requirements.

(Company) prohibits any form of discrimination against any employee, customer, or vendor. Any employee who engages in discriminatory behaviour in their employment will be subject to disciplinary action, up to and including termination.

If you believe someone has violated this policy, please immediately notify your manager and/or the owner. *(Company)* will promptly investigate and take appropriate corrective measures. No employee will be subject to — and *(Company)* prohibits — any form of discipline or retaliation for reporting in good faith incidents of unlawful discrimination or cooperating in any way in the investigation of such reports.

4
Position and Pay

During my time as an HR generalist and manager, I found that the majority of employee inquiries revolved around pay and breaks. If you have an employee handbook that addresses pay, then it becomes easy for the employees to look the information up themselves and answer their own questions. As most of the areas involving pay and breaks are legislated by law, it's a straightforward and useful section to include.

1. Defining Positions

You may or may not want to include a section about positions in your handbook, but it can be helpful if you employ full-time and part-time employees (or seasonal/contract employees). The reason you would want to define different position types is that your benefits coverage would likely be different for your full-time staff versus your part-time or seasonal/contract employees. This should be made clear; Sample 6 is an example of how to explain this in your handbook.

2. Training Pay

You will undoubtedly spend some time training new staff, as well as sending current staff to training sessions during the course of their employment. This can include staff meetings, whether mandatory or not. It's important that your staff know what to expect in terms of paid training time, so include Sample 7.

3. Pay for Travel

Travel for work purposes isn't required in all businesses of course, but if your employees do need to travel for work purposes, then a travel policy is a good idea. It's helpful to state the general travel information you want your employees to have in your handbook, and then have a more detailed travel policy documented elsewhere.

A more detailed document would outline your company's preferred hotels to stay in or car rental agencies to use, food and beverage allowances per day, and address time off for employees who travel for work on the weekends or holidays, for example. You would not necessarily want to include all this detail in your handbook, unless the majority of your staff do travel for work purposes. You will, however, need to customize this policy to your business needs and philosophy while keeping employment standards, overtime, and pay legislation in mind.

You may also want to consider whether or not to offer a per diem, (a small daily amount paid to the employee when the employee is travelling to help cover costs he or she wouldn't normally have at home, such as meals in restaurants), or alternatively whether employees will be allowed to submit receipts for reimbursement rather than you paying a per diem.

If gas and/or vehicle mileage will be covered, the amount is usually revisited regularly by employers and depends on the current costs associated with running and maintaining a vehicle, such as the price of gas. The Canadian Revenue Agency publishes a reasonable per-kilometre allowance, which may be helpful to review.

There is a basic example that you could use for your handbook in Sample 8.

4. Overtime (OT) pay

Overtime (OT) pay is also an area that has different exceptions and rules based on the province in which you operate. Including a general description of OT pay and your policy is important though, as it is a conversation that is bound to be brought up by one of your employees at some point, if it hasn't already been discussed. You will need to go to the employment standards website for your province (listed in section **6.** and available on the CD included with this book) to address specific questions, but in your handbook you should have a section on it. See Sample 9 for an example.

5. Meal Breaks

Your employees will also want to know what your company policy is in regards to their meal breaks. The wording in Sample 10 is very general, so that you can be flexible when it comes to the meal breaks you set. But if your company pays for meal breaks, or has a very specific time during the day when everyone takes their meal breaks, then you should customize the policy to fit your current business.

6. Pay Periods

As the employment standards legislation on pay periods is different in every province, it's important that you follow the laws in the province in which you operate. For example, these are the pay periods that are defined in the employment standards legislation for British Columbia, Alberta, and Ontario:

- **British Columbia:** A pay period may be as long as 16 calendar days, and there must be at least two pay periods in a month. An employer must ensure that employees are paid at least twice a month and within 8 days after the end of the pay period.

- **Alberta:** The maximum pay period that can be used by an employer to calculate earnings is one month. An employer can establish shorter pay periods such as daily, weekly, biweekly, or semi-monthly.

- **Ontario:** Employers must establish a regular pay period and a regular payday for employees.

For more information on your province's pay periods, you can access the employment standards web pages at the following web addresses (which may change without notice):

- Alberta: http://work.alberta.ca/employment-standards.html
- British Columbia: www.labour.gov.bc.ca/esb/
- Manitoba: www.gov.mb.ca/labour/standards/
- New Brunswick: www2.gnb.ca/content/gnb/en/departments/post-secondary_education_training_and_labour.html
- Newfoundland and Labrador: www.gov.nl.ca/lra/faq/labour standards.html
- Northwest Territories: www.ece.gov.nt.ca/advanced-education/employment-standards
- Nova Scotia: http://novascotia.ca/lae/employmentrights/
- Nunavut: www.justice.gov.nu.ca/apps/authoring/dspPage.aspx?page=home
- Ontario: www.labour.gov.on.ca/english/es/
- Prince Edward Island: www.gov.pe.ca/jps/
- Québec: www.cnt.gouv.qc.ca/en/
- Saskatchewan: www.lrws.gov.sk.ca/labour-standards
- Yukon: www.community.gov.yk.ca/es.html

In your handbook, you will want to include a definition of your company's pay periods, so that your employees know when they can expect to be paid. If you are a BC employer and pay your employees biweekly on every other Friday, then you could include a statement such as the one shown in Sample 11.

7. Recording Hours Worked

If you have hourly employees, they will need to know how to record their hours worked and how to submit this to your payroll system. You should include some information on recording their hours worked, such as the text in Sample 12.

8. Report to Work Pay Guidelines

You may want to include a few sentences on reporting to work pay guidelines in your handbook. For example, in BC, an employee who comes to work at the requested time must be paid two hours of work, even if he or she works less than two hours. If the employee was scheduled for more than eight hours and reports to work at the requested time, he or she must be paid for at least four hours. The policy I have included in Sample 13 is very general and would work if you have employees in different provinces. If you have employees in only one province, however, you may want to actually state what the report to work pay guidelines are for your province (these can be found on specific provinces' employment standards web pages).

9. Working from Home or a Remote Location

If working from home or another work location is not an option for your employees, please do not use a section on it. If it is an option, then you will want to include a section on it, such as what is shown in Sample 14.

Sample 6
Defining Positions

Full-time (FT) employee: An employee assigned to 30–40 hours per week. Generally, full-time employees are eligible for all *(Company)* benefit programs, subject to the terms, conditions, and limitations of each benefit program.

Part-time (PT) employee: An employee assigned to less than 30 hours per week. While part-time employees receive all legally mandated benefits under applicable legislation, part-time employees are generally not eligible for any other *(Company)* benefit programs.

Seasonal/contract employee: A FT or PT employee who agrees to work for a temporary period of time. Or, an employee who agrees to work on an "as needed" basis when additional staffing needs occur. While seasonal/contract employees receive all legally mandated benefits under applicable legislation, seasonal/contract employees are generally not eligible for any other *(Company)* benefit programs.

Sample 7
Pay for Training

Time spent in mandatory training is considered working time and is paid. Overtime pay will be applied as required.

Sample 8
Travel Time Pay Guidelines

If you are required to travel for work purposes, you are entitled to be paid for the time spent travelling. Normal travel time to and from work is not considered working time and is therefore not paid, but if you are required to travel to a location other than your normal work site, this may be considered paid work travel time.

For example, Jason normally spends 20 minutes driving to work in the morning, but he was asked to attend a training session at a work site 40 minutes away from his home. While Jason would not be compensated for his 20 minutes of travel time to his normal work location, he will be compensated for his extra 20 minutes of travel time to the training session, as this is excess commuting time for work purposes.

If the company requires that you travel with an overnight stay, please be aware that some of this is paid time, and some of it is unpaid time. Paid time includes the travel time it takes to get to the airport or train station in the morning (minus the amount of your normal commute time), time spent at the airport or train station, and time in the air or on the train. Paid time also includes travel time to the hotel or destination once you have arrived.

For example, Ashley's normal commute time to work is 20 minutes, and it takes her 50 minutes to get to the airport. She will be paid for the additional 30 minutes it takes to drive to the airport. She then has to wait an hour for her flight, and the flight is 4 hours long. She will be paid for these 5.5 hours. Once her flight lands, it takes her another 30 minutes to drive to the convention centre, which she will also be compensated for (for a total of 6 hours' travel time).

Free time while travelling (e.g., time spent shopping, meeting friends or coworkers, or sightseeing) is not considered paid time. Also, once an employee arrives at the hotel, it is unpaid time, the exception being if the employee arrives and then immediately goes to another work site or meeting.

We require that our overtime-eligible employees take their necessary meal and rest breaks when travelling, and attempt to complete their daily travel within 8 hours to avoid overtime.

(Company) offers a per diem of *(insert amount)* for each day spent in a location other than your normal work location when on company business.

Employees required by *(Company)* to use their personal vehicle for work purposes are entitled to reimbursement for such use. For mileage reimbursement, please see our Travel Policy. *(Or, you can include it in your handbook by stating that Company pays $_____/km and gas at a certain rate.)* To receive travel reimbursement, please *(fill in the procedure the employee would need to do, e.g., send his or her manager an email? fill in a form for payroll?)*

Sample 9
Overtime Pay

(Company) recognizes and celebrates that our employees have many interests, hobbies, family, and friends outside of work and we want our employees to lead fulfilled, balanced lives, but there may be times when overtime (OT) work is required and necessary. At *(Company)*, we value our employees' dedication and hard work, but require that employees obtain approval from the *(Manager? Owner?)* before working OT hours. The *(Manager? Owner?)* reserves the right to approve or decline an OT request.

Please note that if you are an employee classified as a manager, under applicable employment standards, you are generally not eligible for OT pay. However, this may differ from province to province.* If you are an employee who is not a manager, you are usually eligible for OT pay in accordance with applicable employment standards.

If you have any questions in regards to whether you are eligible for OT pay or not, please see *(Manager? Owner?)*. For any OT worked by eligible employees, *(Company)* will compensate employees in accordance with applicable employment standards legislation. Time off in lieu of OT pay must be agreed upon in writing by the employee and the *(Manager? Owner?)* before the OT hours have been worked. In every case, all OT hours must be preapproved by the *(Manager? Owner?)* in advance.

*Please note that the job title of "manager" does not necessarily indicate that an employee is a manager under employment standards, and therefore ineligible for OT pay. Employment standards authorities looks at such factors as the nature of work functions, and the level of control and authority in the company. If the employee has the authority to make key business decisions independently (e.g., hiring and firing employees), then he or she is likely OT exempt. Please contact an employment lawyer in your province for more clarification on OT exemptions.

Sample 10
Meal Breaks

At *(Company)*, it's important that our employees take periodic breaks throughout their work day to rest. These breaks are mandated by provincial laws and are usually unpaid. Your manager will advise you of when you can take your break and the duration of your break.

Sample 11
Pay Periods

Pay periods are two weeks long, and begin on a Monday and run through midnight Sunday of the following week. Your pay dates are every other Friday. Pay will include wages for all hours worked up to and including the Sunday before the pay date.

Sample 12
Recording Hours Worked

(Company) complies with applicable provincial legislation regarding pay, but it is also your responsibility as an employee to ensure that your hours worked are recorded properly. The process for recording all your hours worked is *(include it here, e.g., do they fill in a payroll form? Do they clock in and out on the computer? How often do they need to do this? Does the manager/owner need to approve a time sheet before it's submitted?)*

Your diligence in recording your hours worked and submitting them in a timely manner will help us ensure that we pay our employees accurately and on time.

Sample 13
Report to Work Pay Guidelines

An employee may be eligible for minimum daily pay under applicable employment standards if he or she reports to work as requested, but no work is available.

Where there is no specific provincial law on minimum daily pay, then the employee will be paid for the actual hours worked.

Sample 14
Working from Home or a Remote Location

In most cases, an employee will be assigned a work site to report to on a daily basis. Allowing work from home or another remote location will be at the sole discretion of the *(Manager? Owner?)* Employees working from home or from a remote location are required to follow all policies regarding breaks, overtime, and time keeping. Hours worked must be recorded every day.

(Company) will decide what, if any, equipment needs to be supplied to employees for off-site use. All equipment supplied by *(Company)* is the property of *(Company)* and must be returned upon separation of employment from the company.

5
Benefits

In this section we'll cover group and other benefits you may offer your employees.

1. Group Benefits

If your company offers a benefits plan to your employees, whether 100% paid by your company, 100% paid by employees, or somewhere in the middle, then you will want to include this information in your handbook. Group benefits can include extended health and dental coverage, vision coverage, short- and long-term disability, life insurance, and accidental death and dismemberment, to name the most common ones. I will include an example of an explanation of benefits coverage for a handbook in Sample 15, but you will need to customize this section to your own benefits plan.

2. Other Benefits

Whether your company provides a group benefits plan or not, you will likely offer other benefits that will interest your employees and should be communicated to your new staff in particular. For example, do you give employee discounts on your products or services (and if so, what are the rules around purchasing your products or services at the discount you provide)? Do you pay for gym memberships? What about parking spaces? Perhaps you have a contract or agreement with a cell phone provider that will give your employees a discount? I worked with a company that used to buy movie ticket passes at 40% off, and then sell them to their employees at this discounted rate (so they made no profit, but it was a benefit of sorts for employees).

I also worked for a company that bought treats, such as doughnuts and cookies, for their employees every Friday afternoon (in addition to paying for all the coffee, tea, hot chocolate, and milk that their employees wanted to drink). These may seem like small benefits, but when added up can cost an employer a fair amount of money year after year. If you offer these benefits, it is important that your employees know about them! When they are bragging about what a great place your company is to work — which will consequently highlight your company to prospective employees as an employer of choice — they will likely mention the benefits you provide.

Sample 15
Benefits Plan

(Company) feels it is important to be able to offer a benefits plan to our full-time employees for the health and well-being of our employees and their dependants. Here is a general description of what is offered through our benefits plan. For more information, please contact *(benefits provider? your manager?)*

Extended Health, Dental, and Long-Term Disability Insurance

Regular, full-time employees become eligible for group benefits after completing three months of employment at full-time hours.

(Company) pays 50% of the cost of the premium for extended health and dental, and employees pay the other 50%. Employees pay 100% of the premium for long-term disability insurance and, as a result, any benefit paid to employees is non-taxable.

(Company) will deduct the costs of your premiums from your first paycheque every month.

Our plan requires that you must enrol in extended health, dental, and long-term disability if you are benefits-eligible, unless you have coverage elsewhere (i.e., through a spouse or parent). Proof of coverage (within 30 days of being benefits-eligible) that you are under a different plan is required to opt out of our benefits plan.

Life Insurance, Accidental Death & Dismemberment, Short-Term Disability, and in BC, MSP

Regular, full-time employees become eligible for group benefits after completing three months of employment at full-time hours.

(Company) pays 100% of the premium. These premiums are considered taxable benefits and will be shown as additional earnings on your paycheque with taxes withheld:

- In all provinces, life insurance.

- In Québec, accidental death and dismemberment insurance.

- In British Columbia, Group Medical Services Plan (MSP) coverage.

(Your company may have additional benefits that you and/or your employees pay for, such as an Employee Assistance Program, and this should be added here.)

Please fill out a *(benefits provider's name)* form within the first week of starting with *(Company)* and return it to your *(manager? the owner?)* It is your responsibility to inform yourself of the benefits provided and to submit an application form 30 days before you become benefits-eligible. If you do not enrol by your eligibility deadline, your next opportunity to enrol will be when you experience a qualifying life event (e.g., marriage, divorce, losing coverage under your spouse or parents' plan). You must request your enrolment within 30 days after your qualifying life event.

You will receive a benefits card in the mail once you have successfully enrolled in the benefits plan. It is your responsibility to ensure you have been enrolled once you are eligible.

Sample 15 – Continued

Once enrolled, you will need to go onto the *(benefit provider's name)* website to access their claim forms. If you need to file a claim for extended health or dental, please fill in the appropriate form and mail it, along with your receipts, to the address provided on the form. It is our recommendation that you make copies of all receipts being submitted before you mail them. All claims should be filed within one year of being incurred.

If you have any further benefits related questions, you can contact *(benefits provider name)* at *(insert phone number)*, or go to their website at *(insert website address)*.

6
Holidays and Time Away from Work

1. Statutory Holidays

After questions about pay, questions about holiday time and time away from work seem to be the most prevalent, in my experience. Most of these questions can be answered quite simply, as minimum requirements regarding statutory holidays and vacations are governed by provincial employment standards legislation. In your handbook, you will want to include the statutory holiday list for the province(s) in which you operate. I've included a list of the Canadian provinces and territories along with their statutory holidays in Sample 16. For your handbook, you could insert the information only for the provinces in which your business operates.

2. Vacation Policy, Pay, and Eligibility

Vacation time and vacation pay can be very confusing concepts for your employees, as they are two separate and distinct employer obligations. Not to mention that vacation pay and eligibility legislation vary by province, and you probably already created an unofficial vacation policy for your company when you hired your staff. When I started as an HR generalist with a company many years ago, they had given some of their new employees three weeks of vacation time, and others two weeks, because it was what the employees had requested when they signed their offer letters with them. If an employee requested his or her vacation pay without taking vacation time (as he or she wanted the money and not the time off), this company would oblige. And they didn't track any of the vacation time that had been taken by their staff. Needless to say, it caused quite a mess. A clear vacation policy was drafted and communicated to the staff, and we started tracking all vacation time. The grumbling around vacation time and pay ceased, as employees then knew that everyone had to adhere to the same policy.

You will want to spend some time deciding how you want your vacation policy to address vacation time and pay for your employees. I have created a general policy for you to use, that includes the minimum amounts legislated by employment standards, but there are decisions that you will need to make as you are creating it. For exmple, are you only going to offer the minimum required, or do you want to offer more? Should your managers receive more vacation entitlement than your other employees? Do you want to be transparent in your vacation policy so that all staff know how much vacation time they each have, or do you want to keep your managers' allotment of time out of the regular handbook so as to separate this information from the rest of the staff? Do you want to pay out employees' vacation pay with each paycheque instead of paying it out before or during a vacation?

Will you allow your employees to carry over any unused vacation time in excess of statutory minimums, or do they need to use it in the year they accrue it? Is there a time of the year when you do not want your employees to take vacation, that is, will you have a vacation "blackout" period during busy times of the year for your business?

There is a general policy in Sample 17 that you can tailor to your needs and the applicable employment standards in your province. (It is also included on the CD for your use.) Please note that I have included a column for managers' vacation time, but this can easily be removed if you do not want as much transparency in your vacation policy.

3. Other Leaves of Absence

3.1 Pregnancy, parental, or adoption leave

You will likely have an employee apply for pregnancy and/or parental or adoption leave while working for you, if you haven't already. Pregnancy and parental leaves are two different types of leaves, and your employees will need to understand the difference, so that they (and you) can fully prepare for their leave of absence. See Sample 18.

3.2 Compassionate care leave

Employees may need to request leave to care for family. Sample 19 shows two options you could offer your employees. Option A provides the leave with full pay and benefits, while option B provides the leave as prescribed by employment standards (i.e., unpaid). It is your decision as an employer to choose which one fits your company culture best (the sample is also available on the CD, for your use).

3.3 Jury or witness duty or reservist leave

The text in Sample 20 that covers jury or witness duty and reservist leave could be altered for your handbook (it is also available on the CD).

3.4 Family responsibility leave

If you have employees in BC, you will want to add this section. Once again there are two options for you: Option A is where the employer chooses the number of days off with pay (must be a minimum of 5 days), and Option B gives 5 days without pay (keeping in mind that option B is the minimum required by BC Employment Standards); double check with your provincial standards to ensure compliance.

If you have employees in other provinces or territories, check the employment standards for your province. See Sample 21.

3.5 Bereavement leave

For bereavement leave, I have provided three options from which to choose, although you can customize one still if you feel these options don't quite meet your business and company culture needs. Option C, however, is the employment standards minimum for most provinces within Canada (but not all; for example, Yukon provides seven consecutive unpaid days off). You cannot offer less than the employment standards minimum. Your decisions will be whether to provide the leave as a paid leave instead of unpaid leave, whether to offer a few extra days if there is out-of-town travel involved, and whether to allow for additional paid or unpaid days off (over and above the minimum) if the situation warrants it. You will need to consider what you have given your employees in the past who have needed bereavement days, as you may have unknowingly set a precedent. For example, let's say your executive assistant's mother passed away last year, so you gave her two weeks' paid time off to grieve. But now you only want to offer the minimum set out by BC employment standards — three unpaid days — for your staff going forward. You will need to decide how this will be viewed by the rest of your employees when they need to take bereavement leave, as they will undoubtedly remember what you gave to your executive assistant. It's important that your policies are seen as fair and unbiased by your staff, or resentment will build.

See Sample 22; once you have decided on what you would like to offer your employees for bereavement leave, you can choose which option works best for your company and add it in or alter it.

3.6 Other personal leaves of absence

There are other leaves of absence that need to be included in your handbook if you have employees in other provinces. See Sample 23 for sections you may want to add to your handbook.

Not all provinces provide sick day requirements, so if it is not required in your province, it is your decision if this is something you would like to offer your staff (and whether they will be paid or unpaid, or if you'd like to offer more than the minimum days off that are required by law). You will also want to decide if you want to offer any additional unpaid or paid days off under special circumstances. If so, you will need to address questions such as these:

- Who will qualify for additional unpaid or paid days off? Full- and/or part-time staff? Will they need to have worked for your company for a certain period of time before qualifying (one month? three months?)?

- How many extra days will you grant every calendar year, and can the days be broken up or does it need to be a continuous leave? Can the days be carried over to the following year?

- How will you base your decision on whether to grant the leave requests? Will it be based on factors such as length of service, level of responsibility, or job performance? Or will it be based on operational requirements or the reason for the request? Perhaps all of the above?

Employers should be aware that human rights legislation may require an employer to grant a paid or unpaid leave to an employee as part of an accommodation process. In such cases, you may not be able to rely on the strict requirements of your policy and should consult a lawyer. In addition, leaves provided by applicable employment standards legislation cannot be replaced by some other leave structure provided by an employer.

If you do decide to include an additional unpaid personal leave of absence in your handbook, you will also want to include the statement in Sample 24.

Also, if you offer your employees benefits, you will want a statement in regards to how they should manage their benefits before they go on a personal leave. See Sample 25.

Sample 16
Statutory Holidays

(Company) observes the statutory holidays in the province(s) in which it operates. If a holiday falls during your vacation, the time will not count against your vacation time. If the holiday falls on a weekend, the holiday may be observed on another day. Please contact the manager/owner if you have any questions in regards to your statutory holidays.

Alberta
- New Year's Day
- Family Day
- Good Friday
- Victoria Day
- Canada Day
- Labour Day
- Thanksgiving Day
- Remembrance Day
- Christmas Day

BC
- New Year's Day
- Family Day
- Good Friday
- Victoria Day
- Canada Day
- BC Day
- Labour Day
- Thanksgiving Day
- Remembrance Day
- Christmas Day

Manitoba
- New Year's Day
- Louis Riel Day
- Good Friday
- Victoria Day
- Canada Day
- Labour Day
- Thanksgiving Day
- Remembrance Day*
- Christmas Day

New Brunswick
- New Year's Day
- Good Friday
- Canada Day
- New Brunswick Day
- Labour Day
- Remembrance Day
- Christmas Day

Sample 16 – Continued

Newfoundland & Labrador
- New Year's Day
- Good Friday
- Canada Day/Memorial Day
- Labour Day
- Remembrance Day
- Christmas Day

Northwest Territories
- New Year's Day
- Good Friday
- Victoria Day
- National Aboriginal Day
- Canada Day
- First Monday in August
- Labour Day
- Thanksgiving Day
- Remembrance Day
- Christmas Day

Nova Scotia
- New Year's Day
- Good Friday
- Canada Day
- Labour Day
- Remembrance Day**
- Christmas Day

Ontario
- New Year's Day
- Family Day
- Good Friday
- Victoria Day
- Canada Day
- Labour Day
- Thanksgiving Day
- Christmas Day
- Boxing Day

Prince Edward Island
- New Year's Day
- Islander Day
- Good Friday
- Canada Day
- Labour Day
- Remembrance Day
- Christmas Day

Sample 16 – Continued

Saskatchewan
- New Year's Day
- Family Day
- Good Friday
- Victoria Day
- Canada Day
- Saskatchewan Day
- Labour Day
- Thanksgiving Day
- Remembrance Day
- Christmas Day

Québec
- New Year's Day
- Good Friday or Easter Monday (*at Company's option*)
- National Patriot's Day
- St. Jean Baptiste Day
- Canada Day
- Labour Day
- Thanksgiving Day
- Christmas Day

Yukon
- New Year's Day
- Good Friday
- Victoria Day
- Canada Day
- Discovery Day
- Labour Day
- Thanksgiving Day
- Remembrance Day
- Christmas Day

Please note that Boxing Day is not a statutory holiday for any province in Canada except Ontario. It is at the employer's discretion in other provinces and territories as to whether they gift this as a day off to their staff.

*Remembrance Day in Manitoba is not a statutory holiday under employment standards legislation, but it is common practice for employers to pay their employees who do not work on this day. Employees in retail business can also refuse to work on this day if they provide 14 days' notice to their employer. As the employer, you will need to decide on your policy for Remembrance Day in Manitoba, and include it here. Please see Manitoba Employment Standards for more information.

**Remembrance Day in Nova Scotia is not officially a statutory holiday, but an employee who works on Remembrance Day and who has worked on at least 15 of the 30 calendar days immediately before Remembrance Day may be entitled to receive a holiday on another day with pay. Please see the Nova Scotia Employment Standards for more information.

Sample 17
Vacation Policy, Pay, and Eligibility

At *(Company)*, we encourage periods of rest and relaxation for our employees, and we require that you take your allotted vacation time every year.

There is a difference between vacation "time" and vacation "pay." Vacation time is the amount of time off for vacation that you will be allowed to take based on your start date with *(Company)*. Vacation pay is an amount of money based on your previous year's earnings which is intended to be used to cover your needs while on vacation.

The chart below is based on the British Columbia Employment Standards Act and may need to be modified for your province:

When You Are Eligible	Employees	*Managers
Upon hire	Vacation pay: 4% (of the employee's total earnings from the previous year) Vacation time: 2 weeks (after completion of 12 months of employment)	Vacation pay: 6% Vacation time: 3 weeks ***This is an example of what you could offer (an extra vacation time and pay allotment for managers is not required by Employment Standards)**
After 5 consecutive years of employment	Vacation pay: 6% (of the employee's total earnings from the previous year) Vacation time: 3 weeks	Vacation pay: 8% Vacation time: 4 weeks

If you have employees in the province of Saskatchewan, you will want to include the schedule below:

When You Are Eligible	Employees	*Managers
Upon hire	Vacation pay: 6% (of the employee's total earnings from the previous year) Vacation time: 3 weeks	Vacation pay: 8% Vacation time: 4 weeks ***This is an example of what you could offer (an extra vacation time and pay allotment for managers is not required by Employment Standards)**
After 10 consecutive years of employment	Vacation pay: 8% (of the employee's total earnings from the previous year) Vacation time: 4 weeks	Vacation pay: 10% Vacation time: 5 weeks

Sample 17 – Continued

If you have employees in the province of Québec, you will want to include the schedule below:

When You Are Eligible	Employees	*Managers
Québec employees with less than 1 year of service	Vacation pay: 4% Vacation time: 1 day per full month of uninterrupted service, up to a maximum of 2 weeks	Vacation pay: 6% Vacation time: 3 weeks ***This is an example of what you could offer (an extra vacation time and pay allotment for managers is not required by employment standards)**
1 year to less than 5 years of employment	Vacation pay: 4% (of the employee's total earnings from the previous year) Vacation time: 2 weeks	Vacation pay: 6% Vacation time: 3 weeks
5 years of employment and over	Vacation pay: 6% (of the employee's total earnings from the previous year) Vacation time: 3 weeks	Vacation pay: 8% Vacation time: 4 weeks

*Employment standards legislation requires that vacation pay be accrued in a working year (calculated from the date the Employee was first employed) and is paid out to support vacation time taken in the following working year. There may be a variety of ways in which an employer can implement a vacation pay policy, including using a common anniversary date for all employees (a calendar year), paying out vacation pay on each paycheque if the employees so agree in writing, or continuing to pay a salary while an employee is on vacation. Any employee who resigns or is terminated must be paid out the balance of the vacation pay accrued as part of final wages.

Employees should make vacation requests in writing to the *(manager? owner?)* at least *(number of weeks)* in advance (except in cases of emergency) of the requested time off and keep track of their available vacation time when planning their days off. Scheduling vacation time off is at the discretion of the *(manager? owner?)*, acting reasonably, and is based on business needs. If two employees request the same period of time off and only one can be permitted to take the time, generally:

(Choose one of the following for your handbook and remove the others)

OPTION A: the person who requested the time off first will receive the time (first come, first serve basis).

OPTION B: the employee with the most seniority will receive the time.

OPTION C: the manager will decide which employee will receive the time, based on operational requirements.

We will check our employees' vacation balance on a regular basis and encourage our employees to take their vacation time in the year it is accrued. *(Company)* reserves the right to schedule vacation time for its employees if it is not being managed properly by the employee.

Sample 17 – Continued

Other Conditions of Vacation Time and Pay Policy:

- In order to qualify for increased vacation time and vacation pay, an employee's years of service must be continuous. Approved leaves of absence are considered to be continuous service; vacation time is accrued for active and inactive employment but vacation pay is earned on wages. So, while you can earn vacation time while on a leave such as parental leave, your vacation pay for that period will be calculated on any wages you earned during that period.

- Statutory holidays which fall during vacation periods will not count toward vacation time.

- Vacation days are not considered days worked for overtime purposes.

- No payments of vacation pay are offered in lieu of vacation time; the Company will pay eligible employees for unused and accrued vacation pay upon termination of employment.

- In Québec, an employee entitled to two weeks of vacation can request an additional week without pay, but the third week cannot be taken at the same time as the original two weeks and cannot be broken up into separate days throughout the year.

  (You may want to consider these next conditions or variations of these conditions for your vacation policy, based on your business needs and company culture.)

- Employees must use *(all? a minimum of half?)* of their vacation allotment during the calendar year in which it accrues. *(There will be no carryover of vacation amounts, except in special circumstances,* or, *we will allow you to carry over any unused vacation allotment in excess of applicable employment standards with management approval).*

  Note that some employment standards legislation requires employers to ensure that employees take their minimum vacation time each year, so any carryover should only be for any weeks over and above the minimum statutory entitlement.

- Employees may request a vacation time and pay advance up to their annual amount to take time off with pay for what otherwise would have been an approved but unpaid leave of absence. If an employee requests such an advance, the employee will agree, in writing, that if more vacation pay has been received than has been accrued at the time of employee's departure from the Company, any difference will be deducted from the employee's final paycheque to the extent allowed by law.

- The *(manager? owner?)* may approve up to *(number of days)* days of additional *(paid or unpaid?)* time off, once your vacation entitlement has been used for the year. Requests must be made in writing to the *(manager? owner?)*.

- Vacation time can be taken in increments of 4 hours (half days), to allow more flexibility for our employees.

Sample 18
Pregnancy, Parental, or Adoption Leave

It's important to understand the difference between pregnancy and parental leave. Pregnancy (or maternity) leave is an unpaid leave taken by mothers near the end of their pregnancy and/or immediately afterwards. Parental leave is an unpaid leave that can be taken by mothers or fathers to care for their child after the birth or adoption.

Employees who meet the provincial requirements for pregnancy or parental or adoption leave are entitled to take these leaves without pay. The duration of leave and qualifying periods are determined by provincial legislation. Please see the chart below:

Province	Qualifying Period	Length of Pregnancy Leave
Alberta	52 weeks	15 weeks
BC	N/A	17 weeks
Manitoba	7 months	17 weeks
New Brunswick	N/A	17 weeks
Newfoundland and Labrador	20 weeks	17 weeks
Northwest Territories	12 months	17 weeks
Nova Scotia	12 months	17 weeks
Nunavut	12 months	17 weeks
Ontario	13 weeks	17 weeks
Prince Edward Island	20 weeks	17 weeks
Québec	N/A	18 weeks
Saskatchewan	20 weeks	18 weeks
Yukon	12 months	17 weeks

(Company name) requests written notice from its employees 4 weeks* before the proposed commencement of the pregnancy leave with the expected leave and return date. The written notice must attach a medical certificate stating that the employee is pregnant. Please note that *(Company name)* cannot terminate an employee or change a condition of employment as a result of a pregnancy leave.

*Note that minimum notice varies from province to province.

Your benefits during pregnancy leave are as such: *If you have a benefits plan, you will describe which benefits the employee can continue with, such as LTD, extended health and dental, etc. For most benefits companies, they require that the employee decide at the beginning of his or her leave to either continue with or cancel his or her benefits, but this decision cannot be changed during mid-leave. You will probably need to state that the employee will have to pay 100% of his or her share of the premiums for the entire period of his or her leave (by post dated cheque?) otherwise his or her benefits will be cancelled due to nonpayment.*

Employees who do not return to work at the end of their leave are presumed to have resigned, and a Record of Employment (ROE) will be issued.

Sample 18 – Continued

Parental Leave:

Natural or adopting parents may be entitled to parental leave in accordance with provincial employment standards:

Province	Qualifying Period	Length of Parental Leave	Adoption Leave
Alberta	52 weeks	37 weeks	37 weeks
BC	N/A	37 weeks 35 weeks if pregnancy leave is taken	37 weeks
Manitoba	7 months	37 weeks	37 weeks
New Brunswick	N/A	37 weeks	37 weeks
Newfoundland and Labrador	20 weeks	35 weeks	17 weeks
Northwest Territories	12 months	37 weeks	37 weeks
Nova Scotia	12 months	52 weeks 35 weeks if pregnancy leave is taken	52 weeks
Nunavut	12 months	37 weeks	37 weeks
Ontario	13 weeks	37 weeks 35 weeks if pregnancy leave is taken	37 weeks
Prince Edward Island	20 weeks	35 weeks	52 weeks
Québec	N/A	52 weeks	52 weeks
Saskatchewan	N/A	37 weeks 34 weeks if pregnancy or adoption leave is taken	18 weeks
Yukon	12 consecutive months	37 weeks	37 weeks

The birth mother cannot take the parental leave at another time, she must take it immediately after her maternity leave ends. In BC, fathers or adopting parents can take parental leave at any time within 52 weeks of birth or custody. These requirements vary from province to province.

Length of service for mothers and fathers will be deemed to be continuous for vacation time accumulation and other purposes. Please note that while you will accrue vacation time, you do not accrue vacation pay, as you will not have any earnings during your unpaid leave. In BC, Employees will only be paid for statutory holidays if they have worked 15 days out of the 30 days preceding the holiday. These requirements vary from province to province.

Your benefits during parental leave are the same as pregnancy leave, described above.

Employees may be eligible for Employment Insurance benefits during pregnancy and parental leave. Please contact your local Service Canada branch for more information.

Sample 19
Compassionate Care and Emergency Leave

OPTION A: There may come a time when you need to care for a gravely ill family member, and therefore will need to take compassionate care leave. *(Company)* will grant this leave in accordance with applicable employment standards once a medical certificate from a qualified medical practitioner has been reviewed by *(Company)*. This medical certificate needs to state that the family member has a serious medical condition with a significant risk of death within 26 weeks. This is a job-protected leave for up to 8 weeks, but the length varies by province. Employees will be entitled to their full salary and benefits while on compassionate care leave. Please note that this leave can only be used to care for a gravely ill family member, and any extensions given will also be in accordance with provincial legislation.

Please contact the *(manager? owner?)* if you require more information or feel you may need to take a compassionate care leave.

OPTION B: There may come a time when you need to care for a gravely ill family member, and therefore will need to take compassionate care leave. *(Company)* will grant this leave in accordance with applicable employment standards, once a medical certificate from a qualified medical practitioner has been reviewed by *(Company)*. This medical certificate needs to state that the family member has a serious medical condition with a significant risk of death within the following 26 weeks. This is an unpaid, job-protected leave for up to 8 weeks, but the length varies by province (e.g., an employee can take up to 12 weeks in Québec). Please note that this leave can only be used to care for a gravely ill family member, and any extensions given will also be in accordance with provincial legislation.

A decision must be made in regards to your benefits, and whether you want to continue your benefits while on leave. If you decide to continue, you will need to pay 100% of your monthly premiums before you go on leave, in advance or by postdated cheque. If this benefits payment is not paid by the first day of your leave, your benefits will be cancelled for the duration of your leave due to nonpayment.

Please contact the *(manager? owner?)* if you require more information or feel you may need to take compassionate care leave.

(If you have employees in Yukon territory, please be aware of the Critically Ill Child leave, which is an unpaid job-protected leave for employees who have completed 12 months of employment and who are parents to a critically ill child. A medical certificate is required to grant up to 37 weeks to care for and support the ill child.

In addition, some provinces have an emergency or family leave which, although similar in some ways, is distinct from compassionate care leave. Consult your local employment standards legislation for more details.)

Sample 20
Jury or Witness Duty or Reservist Leave

If an employee is required to serve as a witness or jury member (and has received an official notice to do so), he or she is entitled to an unpaid, job-protected leave of absence for the period of time away from work for this purpose.

All provinces across Canada offer some type of unpaid leave for employees who are members of the reserve force, and are deployed overseas or within Canada for an emergency situation. As each province has a different minimum qualification period, please customize the policy below to fit your provincial employment standards.

Employees who are in the reserve force and who are deployed to international operations, or to an emergency operation within Canada, are allowed to take an unpaid, job-protected leave. Employees must be employed with the company for (_____ *consecutive weeks/months)* before they qualify for reservist leave. Employees must also provide reasonable written notice of their leave and return date to their manager/owner.

Sample 21
Family Responsibility Leave BC

OPTION A: Employees are entitled to take up to *(number of days)* paid days off in an employee's employment year, based on start date. This leave is to help employees meet the responsibilities related to the care, health, or education of a child (under the age of 19) in the employee's care, or the health and care of any other member of the employee's immediate family. These days cannot be carried over to the next year(s) if unused. Any time taken off for this purpose during the day (even if it's just one hour) qualifies as one day, unless *(Company)* and the employee agree otherwise.

The request for family responsibility leave does not need to be saved for emergency situations. For example, you may use your family responsibility leave if your child is ill and you need to spend the day at home with him or her, or a parent-teacher conference has been scheduled for the middle of the work day, or you need to take your elderly parent to a doctor's appointment. The employee should give *(Company)* as much advance notice as possible that leave is needed.

OPTION B: Employees are entitled to take up to 5 unpaid days off in an employee's employment year, based on start date. This leave is to help employees meet the responsibilities related to the care, health, or education of a child (under the age of 19) in the employee's care, or the health and care of any other member of the employee's immediate family. These days cannot be carried over to the next year(s) if unused. Any time taken off for this purpose during the day (even if it's just one hour) qualifies as one day, unless *(Company)* and the employee agree otherwise.

The request for family responsibility leave does not need to be saved for emergency situations. For example, you may use your family responsibility leave if your child is ill and you need to spend the day at home with him or her, or a parent-teacher conference has been scheduled for the middle of the work day, or you need to take your elderly parent to a doctor's appointment. The employee should give *(Company)* as much advance notice as possible that leave is needed.

* Family Responsibility leave (or similar leave) is also offered for employees in Manitoba, Ontario, Québec, New Brunswick, Newfoundland and Labrador, and Prince Edward Island, although the requirements of the leave vary by province. Please see your applicable provincial employment standards for more information.

Sample 22
Bereavement Leave

OPTION A: Upon the death of an immediate family member (please see applicable employment standards for a definition of "immediate family member"), *(Company)* will provide *(number of days)* paid, job-protected days off. The days of paid leave do not have to be consecutive and the employee can choose to take fewer than *(number of days)* days. If the employee needs to take additional days off, they may be taken as vacation days. Please contact the *(manager? owner?)* if you are in need of taking bereavement leave.

OPTION B: Upon the death of an immediate family member (please see applicable employment standards for a definition of "immediate family member"), *(Company)* will provide 3 paid, job-protected days off. The days of paid leave do not have to be consecutive and the employee can choose to take fewer than 3 days. If out-of-town travel is required, the company may grant an additional 2 paid days off. If the employee needs to take additional days off, they may be taken as vacation days. Please contact the *(manager? owner?)* if you are in need of taking bereavement leave.

OPTION C: Generally an employee is entitled to 3 unpaid days off upon the death of an immediate family member (please see applicable employment standards for a definition of "immediate family member"). The days of unpaid leave do not have to be consecutive and the employee can choose to take fewer than 3 days. This leave is job protected. If the employee needs to take additional days off, they may be taken as vacation days. Please contact the *(manager? owner?)* if you are in need of taking bereavement leave.

If you have employees in Yukon territory, Manitoba, Nova Scotia, or Newfoundland and Labrador, please be aware of the Disappearance or Death of a Child leave, which grants unpaid leave for an employee whose child has died or disappeared as a likely result of a crime. See applicable employment standards legislation for the length of the leave and qualifying period.

Sample 23
Other Leaves of Absence

Manitoba: Up to 3 unpaid days for personal illness after being employed for at least 30 days.

New Brunswick: Up to 5 unpaid sick days per year if you have been working for your employer for more than 90 days.

Newfoundland and Labrador: Sick leave or family responsibility leave of 7 unpaid days per year.

Northwest Territories: Up to 5 unpaid sick days within a 12-month period.

Nova Scotia: Up to 3 unpaid sick days per year.

Ontario: Personal Emergency Leave of 10 unpaid days in a calendar year for anyone who works for an employer with 50 or more employees, to be used for urgent family matters and illness.

PEI: Up to 3 unpaid sick days for employees who have been with the same employer for 6 months.

Québec: Up to 10 days per year to care for a family member, and providing you have 3 months service with your employer, you can take up to 12 weeks per calendar year to meet obligations resulting from an accident or serious illness of a family member. If you are sick or recovering from an accident, you may take up to 26 weeks leave within a 12-month period.

Saskatchewan: If you have a serious illness or injury, you may be entitled to 12 weeks' unpaid leave per 52-week period, provided you have been with us for a minimum of 13 weeks. If the illness or injury is not deemed very serious, you may be entitled to a leave of not more than 12 days in a 52-week period.

Yukon: Up to 12 unpaid sick days with no carryover year to year, earned at the rate of 1 day per completed month of employment.

(Here are two options you could add to this section if you decide to offer any additional leave of absence days for your staff.)

OPTION A: *(Company)* will provide an extra *(number of days)* paid days off to our *(FT? PT?)* employees who have worked with our company for *(1? 3?)* continuous months. These additional days *(can be broken up and do not need to be used all at once? need to be continuous days off?)*, and *(can/cannot be carried over to the following year)*. These additional days will be granted solely on the basis of factors such as *(length of service/level of responsibility/job performance/operational requirements/reason for the request)*. We reserve the right to grant these days off for these reasons alone: *(sick days/to care for sick children or elderly parents/moving days/study days or days to write exams)*.

OPTION B: *(Company)* will provide an extra *(number of days)* unpaid days off to our *(FT? PT?)* employees who have worked with our company for *(number of months)* continuous months. These additional days *(can be broken up and do not need to be used all at once/need to be continuous days off)*, and *(can/cannot be carried over to the following year)*. These additional days will be granted solely on the basis of factors such as *(length of service/level of responsibility/job performance/operational requirements/reason for the request)*. We reserve the right to grant these days off for these reasons alone: *(sick days/to care for sick children or elderly parents/moving days/study days or days to write exams)*.

Sample 24
No Guarantee

Upon returning to work after completing an approved personal leave of absence that is not a statutory entitlement, you may or may not be reinstated to your original position, or a different position; there is no guarantee of reinstatement, except as may be required by applicable employment standards or human rights law.

Sample 25
Benefits While on Leave

Your benefits, such as your extended health and dental and long-term disability, will continue while you are on your leave.

You are responsible for providing payment for your share of your premiums before you go on leave, by postdated cheque. If payment is not received before you go on leave, coverage will cease.

7
Health and Safety

All provinces in Canada have occupational health and safety regulations governing the workplace, to help prevent employee accidents and disease. These can include requirements to do a violence assessment, to provide training to workers, to provide first-aid attendants, and to create policies and reporting strategies to prevent bullying and harassment. Many large companies are required to establish Joint Health and Safety Committees to ensure workers and their managers are cooperating in creating a safe working environment. Health and safety regulations vary between provinces and territories, but it is your duty as an employer to ensure you are following your provincial health and safety regulations. Please search for the Occupational Health and Safety website for the province in which your company operates, and add the necessary information to your handbook (I have included an example of some of the requirements for BC in Sample 26). Having health and safety information in your handbook is the first step toward helping create a safe working environment, and it shows your company's due diligence regarding your health and safety legal requirements.

While you do not need an extensive section in your handbook about health and safety, please be aware that your company needs to have other documentation in place to be compliant with occupational health and safety regulations (which are dependent on the province in which you operate as well as the industry in which you work). In addition to having your policy information in your handbook, I would recommend compiling a separate safety manual which outlines your duties as an employer; your employees' health and safety responsibilities; information on violence in the workplace; work site inspection reports; information and meeting minutes from your Joint Health and Safety committee meetings (for workplaces with 20 or more employees); and any other training that would be required for your specific industry (e.g., Young Workers at Risk, Ladder Safety, Road Safety). Please see the appropriate legislation for your province to determine your health and safety requirements.

Sample 26
Health and Safety

(Company) is committed to creating a safe environment for its employees. The responsibility for maintaining a safe, hazard-free workspace rests with us, the employer, as well as you, the employee.

As an employee of *(Company)*, you are provided with fundamental health and safety rights while performing your job. These are:

- To be informed of any foreseeable health and safety risks in the workplace.

- To participate in occupational health and safety programs.

- To refuse dangerous work or work that may cause harm, without fear of reprisal from your employer.

How to Report a Workplace Accident or Injury

If an accident, injury, or disease occurs in the workplace, please contact the *(Manager? Owner?)* immediately. You must seek medical attention as soon as possible, and inform the doctor that it is a workplace-related accident, injury, or disease (this includes bullying and harassment that has possibly led to a mental disorder).

(Include the following; edit for your province.)

You will then need to contact WorkSafeBC to start a claim. As an employer, we are given 3 days to submit an Incident and Injury Report to WorkSafeBC, so your immediate notification of a workplace injury is imperative.

To file a report, please contact the Teleclaim Contact Centre at 1-888-WORKERS and they will guide you to the next step and the appropriate form(s) to fill out on the WorkSafeBC website.

Emergency Procedures

Emergencies and disasters can occur at any time, and it's important that we are prepared. In the case of an evacuation, please follow this route out of the building: *(insert directions)*. Our designated assembly area is *(in the parking lot? across the street? in a nearby restaurant or park?)*, where we will gather so that *(Company)* can account for each person.

The location of our fire extinguishers are *(beside each emergency exit door? at the front door? in the warehouse?)*. Our first-aid kit(s) are located in *(insert location)*.*

In case of an evacuation, our first-aid attendant(s) will bring the first-aid kits to the designated assembly area in case anyone is in need of immediate medical attention.

In the event of a disaster, we will communicate with our employees through *(email? telephone? please describe your communication plan)*. Please ensure we always have your most up-to-date contact information in our files.

*You may want to include a floor plan of your building, indicating where the emergency exit doors, fire extinguishers, and fire alarms are.

Sample 26 – Continued

First-aid Information

Occupational Health and Safety laws in each province regulate how many first-aid attendants you must have in your workplace, what level of first-aid training is required, and the types of supplies or equipment needed at your work site.

(In BC, for example, at a low-risk work site that is within 20 minutes' travel time from a hospital, these are the minimum requirements:

Number of Workers per Shift	Supplies/Equipment	Level of First-Aid Certificate for Attendant
1		
2-10	Basic first-aid kit	
11-50	Level 1 first-aid kit	Level 1 certificate
51-100	Level 2 first-aid kit AND a dressing station	Level 2 certificate
101 or more	Level 2 first-aid kit AND a first-aid room	Level 2 certificate

You do not need to include this information in your handbook, but you will want to include some first-aid information if you have two or more employees working for you, such as the following.)

(Company) has *(insert number)* of first-aid kits, located in *(insert locations)*. Our first-aid attendant is *(name)*, *(business title)*, at *(cell number or extension number)*. If you are in need of medical attention, please contact our first-aid attendant immediately. If you are in need of a small medical supply, such as an aspirin or a bandage, you may remove this item yourself from the first-aid kit.

If you are interested in becoming a first-aid attendant for *(Company)*, please contact the *(Manager? Owner?)*.

8
Company Policies

1. Attendance and Punctuality

While you will want to have a few sentences in your handbook on attendance and punctuality, the message and tone of this policy is in your hands to create.

Does your business require that all your employees start at 9 a.m. sharp, no exceptions? Is there shift work involved? Do you have a more flexible business that allows for more casual start and end times? My example in Sample 27 cannot accommodate all of these exceptions, so please tailor this policy to your business requirements.

2. Dress Code or Special Clothing and Personal Hygiene

If your company has a dress code or requires special clothing be worn, then you will need to include a section on this in your handbook. Even if there is no official dress code but you would like to make it clear to your staff that they need to look presentable and professional, then a paragraph in your handbook on your expectations is a must. I have included two different examples: one for a dress code in Sample 28, and one for when a uniform or special clothing is required in Sample 29. Please add in any other information that is specific to your business, such as if you sell product that you would like to encourage your employees to wear.

I have also included Sample 30 about personal hygiene. You may think it is excessive to cover this, but it is better to put something in the handbook up front than have to deal with an employee who wears so much perfume it irritates someone with an allergy later.

3. Job Abandonment

It is a good idea to include something about job abandonment in your handbook. It's unfortunate, but sometimes employees will "resign" from their jobs and won't show up for work, without letting you know they are doing so. You will be happy to have a written policy in place if that occurs. See Sample 31.

4. Professional Conduct and Possible Reasons for Termination

This policy, while possibly appearing overly serious, is an important one to have in your handbook. While 99% of your staff might never conduct themselves in an unprofessional manner, there could be that one employee who will push the boundaries of professional conduct, and who may even do something illegal. You are doing your due diligence as an employer to have a policy that addresses how unprofessional conduct will be dealt with at your company. Once this has been established, it's important that you maintain consistent disciplinary actions for all your staff, as you will be establishing a precedent for how your company deals with unprofessional conduct. See Sample 32.

5. Technology Use Policy

Technology use brings with it special challenges including laying out policies for how employees represent your company on social media, and how they are allowed (or not allowed) to use the company's computers, Internet, email, and other resources. Use Sample 33 but alter it for your company.

6. Drug- and Alcohol-Free Workplace

Include a policy for your company about keeping drugs and alcohol away from the workplace such as what is shown in Sample 34. This is not a comprehensive policy, and you should be aware that employers are subject to a number of human rights obligations which may impact how this policy can be implemented. You should have your policy reviewed by a lawyer in your province.

7. Non-Disclosure Agreement

Include a non-disclosure agreement like the one in Sample 35 to remind employees they are not to share company information or trade secrets.

Sample 27
Attendance and Punctuality

It is imperative to our business that you are respectful of your work schedule. Your attendance and punctuality are extremely important; when you do not show up for work on time, then your fellow employees have to bear the burden of your absence, and our clients may suffer as a result.

As a general rule, our work day runs from 8:00 a.m. to 5:00 p.m., with a half-hour unpaid break for lunch and two 15-minute, unpaid coffee breaks. If you are going to be late or absent, please call your manager as far in advance as possible. If you are absent due to sickness, your manager may ask you for a doctor's note.

If you fail to notify your manager of your lateness or absence, you may be subject to disciplinary action, up to and including termination.

Sample 28
Dress Code

We at *(Company)* expect our employees to dress in a neat, clean, professional manner. Specifically, we do not allow shorts, tank tops, or open-toed shoes to be worn at any time. All clothing is to be neat looking (i.e., wrinkle free with no rips or holes). It is important that you exemplify our business and culture every day that you are at work, and that you project this image to our clients.

Your appearance and personal hygiene are important to you and everyone around you at work. Please be sensitive to the fact that people have different allergies/sensitivities to colognes and perfumes, body odour and the smell of smoke on your clothes.

If an employee comes to work dressed in an unprofessional manner or with unacceptable personal hygiene, he or she may not be allowed to start work for the day and will be sent home (and will only be paid for the time he or she has worked). Failure to adhere to our dress code policy may result in disciplinary action, up to and including termination.

If you have any questions about what is or isn't appropriate to wear to work, please ask *(Manager? Owner?)*.

Sample 29
Special Clothing

At *(Company)*, we require that you wear shirts with our company logo on them every time you are working. This helps our employees connect with our customers and project an air of expertise, while helping our customers easily identify who our employees are. Therefore we will provide three shirts to every new employee before the start of their first shift. These shirts are the responsibility of the employee to keep neat and clean, free of holes or rips. We will provide 2 new replacement shirts every 6 months.

To keep your shirts clean and professional looking, you may have them dry cleaned as often as required, and submit the dry cleaning receipt to your manager for reimbursement. We encourage our employees to wear khaki pants or black pants with our shirts, to maintain a professional looking appearance. Skirts and shorts are not allowed.

Sample 30
Personal Hygiene

Your appearance and personal hygiene are important to you and everyone around you at work. Please be sensitive to the fact that people have different allergies/sensitivities to colognes and perfumes, body odour, and the smell of smoke on your clothes.

If an employee comes to work with unacceptable personal hygiene, he or she may not be allowed to start work for the day and may be sent home (and will only be paid for the time worked). Failure to adhere to our personal hygiene policy may result in disciplinary action, up to and including termination.

Sample 31
Job Abandonment

If you fail to show up to work for *(3 consecutive days/shifts?)* in a row, without contacting your manager, then you may be deemed to have abandoned your job or voluntarily terminated your employment with *(Company)*, subject to compliance with applicable human rights law.

Sample 32
Professional Conduct and Termination

(Company) expects that all of its employees will conduct themselves in a manner that protects our business, our reputation, and the health and safety of our staff and clients. An employee who conducts himself or herself in a way that does not meet our accepted policies and practices may be subject to disciplinary action, up to and including termination.

The following is a list of examples of unacceptable behaviour that may result in disciplinary action, but by no means does this encompass all examples of misconduct:

- Theft or misuse of company intellectual property or information.

- Violation of company policies.

- Harassment, bullying, discrimination, or retaliation against our employees, clients, or vendors.

- Failure to report to work and/or tardiness.

- Failure to perform job duties or responsibilities.

- Acting in an offensive manner.

- Any illegal activities while at work.

Disciplinary action is designed to help correct an employee's performance or conduct, and can take many different forms, including but not limited to verbal and written warnings, suspension (with or without pay), demotion, and termination. *(Company)* generally adheres to a policy of progressive discipline, whereby a first offence may call for a verbal warning, a next offence may result in a written warning, and further offences may call for suspensions or termination. Not all steps will be followed in all cases, and *(Company)* reserves the right to decide on the level of disciplinary action for each situation.

(Company) may terminate an employee's employment for serious misconduct, without warning, advance notice, or compensation.

Sample 33
Technology Use

Technology, including computer facilities and infrastructure, is provided to our employees so they can do their jobs. The equipment, services, and technology that employees use to access the Internet are always the property of *(Company)*. Therefore, you should have no reasonable expectation of privacy and *(Company)* reserves the right to monitor Internet traffic. We also reserve the right to retrieve and read any data that is composed, sent, or received through our online connections or is stored in our computer systems. Those using Company-provided technology must respect the intellectual property rights of others. Employees should be aware that any use of the facilities or infrastructure that is in violation of the guidelines listed below may lead to disciplinary action, up to and including termination.

Network Security

It is important to protect the privacy and security of *(Company)*'s information, as well as our employees' and clients' information. Here are some examples of activities that are NOT allowed:

- Unauthorized attempts to gain privileged access or access to any account or computer not belonging to you on any Company computer or system.

- Creation of any program, Web form, or other mechanism that asks for a Company user identity and password.

- Sharing accounts or passwords.

- Knowingly running or installing on any computer system or network, or giving to another user, a program intended solely for the purpose of damaging or placing excessive load on a computer system or network.

Each user is responsible for the proper use of his or her account and any activity conducted with it. This includes choosing safe passwords and protecting them.

Each computer user is responsible for the security of any computer he or she connects to the network. A computer seen to be attacking other systems (e.g., having fallen victim to viruses/worms or similar) will be taken off the network, generally without notice, until it has been made secure.

Any user who finds a virus or other possible security lapse on any Company system must report it to the system administrator. To protect your files and the system, do not attempt to use any computer which may be infected until the system administrator has investigated the problem.

Computer Usage Policies

No Company computer may be used for purposes that violate Company policies or provincial and/or federal law.

Be mindful that many people use Company computers for daily work. Obstructing this work by consuming gratuitously large amounts of system resources (disk space, CPU time, print quotas, network bandwidth) or by deliberately crashing computers will not be tolerated. Please co-operate by running large jobs on shared systems at off-peak hours.

Sample 33 – Continued

Use of any Company computer by outside individuals or organizations requires special permission from the system administrator.

Use of Company computers for commercial purposes other than those of the Company, except where explicitly approved, is strictly prohibited.

No Company computer may be used for playing computer games.

Copying, storing, displaying, or distributing copyrighted material using Company computers or networks without the express permission of the copyright owner, except as otherwise allowed under the copyright law, is prohibited.

Copying, storing, displaying, or distributing pornographic material using Company computers is prohibited. This prohibition extends to using Company computers to view websites displaying such material.

Internet Access

Internet access is provided to staff to enable them to undertake Company business. Use of the Internet for personal reasons should be of limited and infrequent duration, and this privilege may be withdrawn if such use is considered excessive.

(Company) reserves the right to block user access to specific websites, or groups of websites, without notice to staff.

(Company) reserves the right to track and log Web access, including sites visited.

Staff are prohibited at all times from using *(Company)*'s computers for shopping, trading in stocks, shares, or other negotiable instruments, or participating in online auctions.

Email Usage

Any email sent from a Company computer is the property of the Company, not the employee, and therefore employees should not have expectations that their emails are private and confidential.

No email may be sent or forwarded through a Company computer for purposes that violate Company policies or provincial and/or federal law.

In accordance with the Company's Discrimination, Harassment, and Bullying Policy, nuisance email or other online messages such as chain letters, obscene, harassing, or other unwelcome messages are prohibited. This includes using computers or email to act abusively toward others or to provoke a violent reaction, such as stalking, acts of bigotry, threats of violence, or other hostile or intimidating "fighting words." Such words include those terms widely recognized to victimize or stigmatize individuals on the basis of race, ethnicity, religion, sex, sexual orientation, disability, and other protected characteristics.

Unsolicited email messages to multiple users are prohibited unless explicitly approved by the appropriate department head. All messages must show accurately from where and from whom the message originated. Inappropriate mass mailing or talk requests such as multiple mailings to newsgroups, mailing lists, or individuals (e.g., "spamming," "flooding," "blogging," "bombing," or "snerting") are serious violations of Company policy.

Sample 33 – Continued

The Company reserves the right to refuse mail and other connections from outside hosts that send unsolicited, mass, or commercial messages, or messages that appear to contain viruses to Company or other users, and to filter, refuse, or discard such messages.

Software policy

It is the policy of *(Company)* to respect all computer software copyrights and to adhere to the terms of all software licenses to which the Company is a party. *(Company)* employees and others working on behalf of the Company (such as independent contractors) may not:

- Duplicate any licenced software or related documentation for use either on Company premises or elsewhere without obtaining written permission from the system administrator and then only provided the Company is expressly authorized to duplicate the software by agreement with the licensor.

- Use software on multiple machines or local area networks unless authorized by *(Company)*'s licence agreements.

- Give software used by the company to any third parties, including contractors and customers.

- Use or install on any Company computer system any software that has not been provided by Company or approved in writing by the system administrator. Any personal software approved for use shall be registered with the system administrator and shall be recorded as personally owned. Approval may be withheld by the system administrator for any reason. In the event the system administrator believes, in his or her sole discretion, that approved software may harm computer equipment, is improperly licensed or is infected by a computer virus, the system administrator may direct the employee or contractor to remove the software from Company's computer equipment and the employee shall comply with such direction.

  All software acquired by the Company must be purchased by the system administrator. Software acquisition is restricted to ensure that the Company has a complete record of all software that has been purchased for Company computers and so that it can register, support, and upgrade such software. The Company will not provide support for software that has not been approved for purchase pursuant to the terms of the Company Computer Software Policy.

  Unauthorized duplication of software may subject employees and/or the Company to both civil and criminal penalties under applicable provincial and/or federal law.

Violations of these policies may result in the immediate suspension of an employee's computer account and network access privileges pending investigation of circumstances. Violations of these policies may lead to discipline up to and including termination.

If you have any questions in regards to the Technology Use Policy, please contact *(IT? Manager? Owner?)*

Sample 33 – Continued

Social Media Policy

For the purposes of this policy, social media refers to, but is not limited to, blogs, wikis, Twitter, Facebook, YouTube, LinkedIn, and Flickr. This policy is in addition to, and complements, our current and any future policy on our computers, technology, and the Internet.

While we understand and support that our employees want to share their opinions and talk about their work with their friends, family, and community, please know that it is not acceptable to publish confidential company information. This could include financial reports, trade secrets, new product information, and details about a confidential project. Disclosing confidential information on social media may lead to discipline, up to and including termination. If you are unsure of what information you can share and what you can't, please err on the side of caution and don't share it!

We feel that honesty and transparency are the best policy, so if you post about the Company, please disclose who you are and that you work for *(Company)*. Do not blog anonymously or under false identities. We know that you have a point of view and encourage you to share it, but also encourage you to keep in mind that you are a company representative, and are expected to act with the company's best interest in mind. Disparaging or insulting comments about *(Company)* are not acceptable, and any language that is harassing or defamatory is prohibited.

It's important to also be respectful of *(Company)* copyrights, trademarks, and logos. You must ask permission before you use these on your social media channels.

In general, use your best judgment, and make it very clear that your opinions are yours alone and do not represent the Company's official views. Always consider the consequences of what you have written, as it can and will be seen by your boss, your clients, your vendors, and your coworkers. Saying anything that will embarrass or insult our customers or our business will lead to disciplinary action, up to and including termination.

Any after-hours use of social media for work purposes needs to be pre-approved by your manager, as this may be considered paid work time. For example, if your manager has asked you to take pictures of a new product and upload it to the website when you get home, this would be considered paid work time.

If you have any questions in regards to social media and what is acceptable to publish, please contact *(Manager? IT? Marketing?)*.

Sample 34
Drug- and Alcohol-Free Workplace

We at *(Company)* want to provide a safe, healthy environment for all of our employees. To help maintain this goal, we have a strict policy against the use of alcohol and the unlawful use of drugs in the workplace. Our drug- and alcohol-free workplace policy applies whenever someone is working at, representing, or conducting business with *(Company)*.

The consumption, use, sale, purchase, transfer, or possession of illegal drugs (or the consumption or use of alcohol) at any time while on *(Company)*'s premises, in company vehicles, or on job sites, or while representing or conducting business on behalf of the Company, is strictly prohibited.

Any employee reporting to work with illegal drugs (or their metabolites) or alcohol in his or her bodily system, or with the odour of alcohol or illegal drugs on his or her breath or body, will be in violation of this policy.

"Illegal drug" means any drug not obtained legally, whether a prescribed substance (but not being used as prescribed or by the person prescribed), or not a prescribed substance.

(Company) encourages individuals to voluntarily seek help with drug and alcohol problems.

(If your company wants to include a section on assistance, then you could add a few sentences, such as: [Company] recognizes that drug and alcohol addiction are treatable diseases and we want to support our employees through the rehabilitation process as much as we can. Therefore, we encourage our staff to seek help with qualified professionals if they are concerned that they have a drug or alcohol addiction. We offer our employees with drug and alcohol problems [support through our group benefits program? support by allowing our employees to use their accrued sick days/vacation days/unpaid days?] while seeking treatment. Treatment for alcoholism and/or other drug use disorders may be covered by the employee benefit plan. However, the ultimate financial responsibility for recommended treatment belongs to the employee.)

Occasional exceptions to this policy in regards to moderate alcohol consumption may be made at *(Company)*'s sole discretion, generally during company sponsored social events. At these events, employees are expected to exercise good judgment in regards to their alcohol consumption. Employees are expected to comply with all legislation regarding prohibiting the use of motor vehicles while under the influence of alcohol, and to take all safety precautions, including arranging for a safe transfer home.

Violation of our drug- and alcohol-free workplace policy is very serious, and will result in disciplinary action, up to and including termination.

Sample 35
Non-Disclosure

In the course of employment with *(Company)*, employees may be privy to valuable confidential information and trade secrets. Employees are to treat such information as confidential and to take all necessary precautions to not disclose such information to third parties.

9
Other Information

1. If You Voluntarily Leave the Company

Sample 36 shows some text you can alter about employees who leave your employ.

2. Changes to Your Personal Information

It's a good idea to ask employees to tell you of changes to their lives that may affect the company in some way in the future, such as when you want to contact them. See Sample 37.

3. Any Other Company-Specific Policies

This is the section in which you should address any other policies that are specific to your company. For example, perhaps you offer an employee referral bonus program, or sabbatical leaves for your long-term employees.

You will want to take a moment to think about any unofficial policy that is part of your company culture, and decide if you would like to make it official. It was unofficially known at one company I worked for that the owner would pay for any employee's marathon entry fee, and the owner would join the employee during the run, because he loved to run marathons. When we sat down to write his employee handbook, we decided to make it an official policy that his company would pay for any sporting-related race fee for his staff, not just for marathons, to help promote the company's culture of health and fitness. This way it was not an underground, word-of-mouth concept that current employees would sometimes mention to new employees. It was a very clear policy to which everyone had access and knew the rules. It became an exciting part of company culture, as the employees would form teams and compete against each other on race days.

Sample 36
Leaving the Company

If you decide to leave *(Company)* voluntarily, we wish you well in your future endeavours, but we do request that you give at least two weeks' written notice. Written notice gives us the opportunity to provide a smooth transition of your duties.

On your last day, all company equipment must be returned to the company. This includes, but is not limited to, keys, laptops, cell phones, and training or development materials. Please note that if you fail to return company equipment to the company, the cost of the equipment may be deducted from your final paycheque.*

*Note that provincial employment standards laws require that any deductions from wages be expressly authorized by the employee in writing. You can include such clauses in an employment agreement. It is best to be as specific as possible about the times in which the employer can deduct or withhold any wages.

(If your company conducts exit interviews, you can add:) *(Company)* will also schedule an exit interview with you before your last day. This information is important for us to grow and improve. Your feedback, which is greatly appreciated, is necessary to help us accomplish this.

It is *(Company's)* policy in regards to giving references to only verify our employees' titles and dates of employment. Any information about the employee, including salary verification, will only be given once the employee submits a request in writing to *(Manager? Owner?)*.

Sample 37
Personal Information

Life events can and will occur on a regular basis — marriage, divorce, new baby, moving houses — and when these occur it is important that you notify us of the change.

In particular, any change of address, phone number, or emergency contact number needs to be updated in our employee file so that we always have a way of contacting you. Other changes, such as marriage or a birth, will likely impact your benefits coverage, and therefore you will want to notify us so we can notify our benefits carrier as soon as possible after the life event has occurred.

10
Not Quite the End

Congratulations! By working through this book and adapting the samples from the CD to suit your business, you have created your employee handbook. But, this does not mean that your work is done for good. HR policies and legislation do evolve and change, along with your own company's policies and practices. As a general rule, I would recommend reviewing and updating your handbook once a year, to ensure it remains relevant.

Now that you have your handbook finished, how are you going to distribute it to your staff? Are you going to plop it down on their desks on Monday morning and tell them all to read it, or are you going to give it the attention it rightly deserves? If you roll it out to your staff in a way that tells them this is important, then they will treat it as important. I recommend scheduling a company meeting and distributing the handbooks to your staff when you are all together (and perhaps going over some of the policies you find the most key to your business).

I suggest asking employees to take the following week to read it, sometime during working hours as this should be done on paid work time, and come to the next meeting with any questions they may have. Ask them to sign their Acknowledgements, (found at the end of Sample 1 in Chapter 1 of this book), make a copy of it, and bring it to the next meeting. This way, when you meet again in a week's time, you can address any issues or questions your staff may have as they will have had time to process what they have read. Ensure you take a copy of their signed Acknowledgements and tell them to keep the other copies in their own handbooks.

An employee handbook can be a wonderful tool for decreasing communication errors and increasing employee productivity, but it cannot replace person-to-person conversations. This handbook is a first step toward creating those conversations with your employees, and making it clear that they can address any issue with you, at any time (i.e., your door is always open). Once your employees have a clearly written handbook on your company policies and understand the topics that you have addressed, you will be surprised that the people issues that you once had to deal with on a daily basis will start to dwindle, allowing you more time to focus on your growing business.

The CD included with this book offers all the policies covered in this book for you to use and modify for your own employee handbook, as well as a list of (current at time of writing) URLs for provincial employment standards websites across the country.

OTHER TITLE OF INTEREST FROM SELF-COUNSEL PRESS

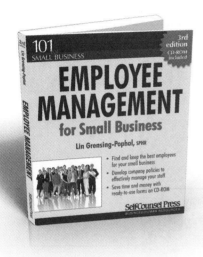

Employee Management for Small Business

Lin Grensing-Pophal, SPHR
ISBN: 978-1-55180-863-5
Suggested retail price: $23.95 CAD

Whether a business has 1 or 100 employees, *Employee Management for Small Business* provides the tools and knowledge required to take an active and positive approach to maintaining an effective human resources plan.

Finding and keeping good employees is crucial to the success of every business, but it s not easy. This book will show small-business owners how to develop a human resources plan tailored to their needs.

From hiring and orientation to developing company policies and negotiating employment contracts, this book covers the essentials of employee management.

Like all the books in the *101 for Small Business* series, each topic in the book is explained in simple language and is illustrated with real-world examples, checklists, and forms.

The Author

Lin Grensing-Pophal has written many business and employee management articles for general and trade publications, and is the author of several books published by Self-Counsel Press. She is accredited through the International Association of Business Communicators and the Society for Human Resource Management, and is a member of the American Society of Journalists and Authors.